SUFFICIENT GRACE:

Faith Walking Through Adversity

BY: TAMEKA L. JOYNER

DEDICATION

To Keshon, Shakina, and my grandchildren, Kayden and Riley, you are the reasons I strive to be great. I thank God for blessing me with each of you because you make me want to be the best mother and grandmother I can be. May your testimony be "because of Momma's obedience, our generation is blessed."

To my family and friends who have encouraged me along the way, thank you for your prayers, support, and love through this process. You were there in sickness and in health. I know that at times I was not the easiest person to care for, but you guys loved me and stood by my side anyway. For that, I'm grateful.

To my "circle" that's forever changing and growing, it is a blessing to be surrounded by a group of genuine go-getters who are not afraid to be great for God. Thank you for pushing and sometimes dragging me toward my purpose.

Momma, I love you. I'm the woman I am today because of the woman who raised me. You taught me how to fight, as well as the art of survival. You have always been a caretaker with a huge heart for people. Thank you for being you.

Daddy, I love and miss you dearly. I told you that your baby girl would be okay.

TABLE OF CONTENTS

INTRODUCTION

My life has been full of difficulties.

At a young age I was set apart.

I began losing my hair when I was 7 years old.

My mom didn't know what was causing it, and a doctor suggested it could be a condition caused by nerves. Children can be really mean. I was picked on daily and had to deal with bullies from elementary through my high school years. If that wasn't enough, at 19 I was diagnosed with systemic lupus erythematosus, also known as "lupus."

At times I felt like life dealt me a bad hand. Why could I not be a normal girl? Why did I have to lose my hair and feel like an outcast? Why did I have to suffer from a chronic disease? I didn't know why God chose me to go through such adversity, and I honestly felt like I was at my breaking point.

Through a failed marriage, several diagnoses, surgeries, feelings of hopelessness, anger, fear, rejection, despair, and depression, He was there. It has taken me years to realize that God had a plan to turn all of this around for my good.

In 2009 I accepted Jesus as my Lord and Savior. This walk has not been easy, but my life is being restored and His power is evident.

I've learned that God has a way of crafting certain circumstances in our lives that reveal gifts He placed deep inside of us. He is God, and He knows exactly what it will take to get those gifts out of each of us.

God can and will use adversity to reveal the true state of our hearts and build our character, patience, and faith. He will also use it to build our testimony. All that I have gone through has been painful and there have been plenty "Why me?" moments.

Now I understand why.

This book is written with three people in mind. The first person is the one who is not currently in a storm. I want to share with you the importance of knowing your identity in Christ before adversity hits.

The second person is the one in the middle of a storm. I want to encourage you to stand firm and hold on to the promises of God. This is a daily walk. With every step you make forward, your faith will grow. I want you to come out of this storm with your faith still intact.

The third person is the one who has made it to the other side. I want to empower you to share your story of how you made it through. I pray that this book causes a ripple effect in your lives. May you come out of your trial as pure gold.

Prayer: Father, I thank you for my brothers and sisters reading this book. I pray that you strengthen them during their trials and that their faith does not waver. I pray that, as they turn the pages of this book, your Holy Spirit opens their hearts to the truth of the Gospel. I pray that the captives are set free, the sick are healed, and the bound are delivered, in Jesus' name.

Amen.

CHAPTER 1

ADVERSITY VS. IDENTITY

Nothing can have you questioning your identity like adversity. Our lives may seem to be going just fine, then all of a sudden life throws a curveball and everything around you has changed. When the dust finally settles, who are you? Well, I can tell you who you're not. You are not what has happened or is happening to you. What if I were to tell you that some storms are assigned to our lives to build our character and reveal our purpose? Ultimately, God will use these same storms to strengthen our faith-walk with Him. You will never know how much faith you have until you've been tested on what you say you believe about yourself and about God. There was a time when I thought my identity was wrapped up in what was happening to me. Since I didn't know who I was, one was given to me. When I was told that I had lupus, it not only became my reality, but I allowed it to become my identity.

My sisters and I were asked to represent the Lupus Foundation at the Annual St. Patrick's Day Parade in a nearby city, and we were beyond excited. When we arrived at the meet-up spot, some of us were given beads and candy to throw out to those along the parade route, while others of us were given signs to carry. Most of the signs had statistics about lupus, but not mine. My sign was on a bright green poster that read "I AM THE FACE OF LUPUS" in bold black letters. At the time I thought nothing of it, and soon the parade began. I walked down the street holding this sign smiling and waving proudly at the crowd. I was so excited that I was helping spread awareness about the disease that was affecting me and millions of others. A few days later, I began receiving photos from the parade and there it was, a close-up of me proudly holding that sign. As I sat and stared at the picture, my smile turned into a look of disgust. The light bulb came on, and immediately I thought, "Wait a minute, that's not who I am." How in the world did I get here? I had been given a label and for years allowed my life to become consumed in being "the woman with lupus" and "Tameka, the Super Lupus Advocate." Allow me to educate you a little about this disease that was part of my life for over 20 years. Lupus is a chronic autoimmune disease that can damage any part of the body (skin, joints, and/or organs). "Chronic" means that the signs and symptoms tend to last for months or even many years. With lupus, something goes wrong with the immune system, which is the part of the body that fights off viruses, bacteria, and germs ("foreign invaders," like the flu). Normally, our immune systems produce proteins called "antibodies" that protect the body from these invaders. "Autoimmunity" means your immune system cannot tell the difference between these foreign invaders and your body's healthy tissues ("auto" means "self"). As a result, it creates autoantibodies that attack and destroy healthy tissues. These autoantibodies cause inflammation, pain, and damage in various parts of the body. Now, tell me again, why in the world would anyone in their right mind want to be the face of something so ugly? I had signed up to be the poster child for infirmity. I was upset with myself and became determined to find out exactly who I was because, clearly, this was not it.

If you have found yourself being wrapped up in an identity of what has happened to you, a diagnosis you were given, or a mistake you made, I have great news: you can allow the Word of God to redefine you. We live in a microwave culture where we want immediate results, but some things take time. This is a process, not a quick fix. There are several steps we must take in order to begin to discover our true identity.

Step 1: Change Your Thinking

1 Peter 4:12-13 says "Beloved, do not be surprised at the fiery trial when it comes upon you to test you, as though something strange were happening to you. But rejoice insofar as

you share Christ's sufferings, that you may also rejoice and be glad when his glory is revealed."

I'm not suggesting that you ignore what's happening to you. However, I am suggesting that you think differently about your circumstances. Perception is a belief or opinion based on how things seem. We are called to walk by faith and not by sight. Even when we don't see God moving in our situation, we have to have the faith to know He is still there and concerned about us. You either believe God has a plan for this to work out for your good or that it won't.

Step 2: Believe that God Loves You

Psalm 46:1 says "…Fear not, for I have redeemed you; I have called you by your name; You are Mine. When you pass through the waters, I will be with you; And through the rivers, they shall not overflow you. When you walk through the fire, you shall not be burned, Nor shall the flame scorch you. For I am the Lord your God, The Holy One of Israel, your Savior…"

We must accept the fact that God loves us unconditionally.

He knows and loves the real you with morning breath and crust in your eyes.

The you without makeup.

The one with the tear-stained face.

The you who is fearful and full of insecurity.

There is nothing you can do to make Him love you any more or any less. Don't you know that you are a one-of-a-kind design? He knew that there was someone who will need your experiences to be able to get through theirs. God desires for you to believe that you are enough--just as you are.

Nothing extra is needed or required. We must find our identities in Him, not what has or is happening to us. We need to be reminded that our adversity is not our identity. You are not the face of any illness or circumstance. Remember that we cannot allow the storm to define our identity.

Instead, choose to allow it to reveal your identity.

Step 3: Daily Affirmations

What are you saying about yourself?

When we say things like, "I'll never get over this" or "Bad things always happen to me," we're basically speaking those things into existence.

We must be careful of our words because they have the power to bring life or cause death. There is a heart-to-mouth connection.

That means our words reveal what's really in our hearts. Our words are supposed to encourage, edify, and bring hope. We must learn to speak life over ourselves before we can speak life to others.

When was the last time you gave yourself a pep talk?

I encourage you to try it today.

Stand in front of your mirror, smile, and say, "I can. I will. I must get through this!"

Do this every day until it sinks in and you start to believe it. Begin today using "I am" statements.

I have to remind myself daily that "I am chosen. I am equipped. I am fearless. I am loved. I am accepted. I am valuable."

CHAPTER 2

❦

FIX YOUR FOCUS

John 11:4 states, "But when Jesus heard it he said, 'This illness does not lead to death. It is for the glory of God, so that the Son of God may be glorified through it.'"

I would be lying if I told you that I have always walked around as this "Super Christian" who's afraid of nothing and is always the image of strength and courage.

Believe me, I'm far from it.

At the age of 33, I was undergoing my second total hip replacement in five years.

I was prescribed high doses of prednisone to treat lupus flares, which led to a condition called avascular necrosis. This condition is when the ball and socket joint in the hip deteriorates, causing excruciating pain. At this point I was sick and tired of being sick and tired.

I was tired of pain.

I was tired of waddling like a duck.

I was tired of walkers.

I was tired of canes.

I was tired of doctors.

I was tired of nurses.

I was tired of people, period.

I WAS TIRED!

I wanted to lock my bedroom door, curl up in the fetal position, and be left alone forever. It was like one diagnosis turned into an avalanche of problems, and whatever treatments the doctors tried just ended up in more negative reactions. I was at my wits' end. Negative report after negative report coupled with what seemed like never-ending pain had me ready to wave a white flag of surrender because I was over it all.

While in the hospital a few days after hip surgery, my anesthesia had finally worn off enough for me to be able to comprehend what was going on around me. I had taken my Bible with me and was reading one of my favorite passages in the book of John where Jesus had been told that his friend Lazarus was sick.

I came upon John 11:4: "But when Jesus heard it he said, 'This illness does not lead to death. It is for the glory of God, so that the Son of God may be glorified through it.'"

Something in me quickened.

It was like a lightning bolt went through my body, so I read it again. I started to get excited and read it one more time out loud, and it was like the words were illuminated on the page.

I knew right then that God was there and was speaking to me.

I felt a release.

At that moment, all of those emotions that were bottled up were released in a flow of steady tears.

Somehow, I knew that I would be OK. God knew how to speak to that deep place of frustration and bring me comfort in knowing that He had a plan to get glory out of this sickness.

Here I sit 10 years later, and that sickness (lupus) did not kill me. Instead, it was the catalyst that propelled me into the will of God to bring Him glory.

I could no longer play the victim to this diagnosis, but I had to choose to fight for my life. Although everything around me was changing, I could not allow it to defeat me.

Once I began to think differently, I began to act differently. Just like Lazarus, I got up out of my condition and began to live again. We're each given a choice to live or die. It sounds like a simple choice, but we can easily say we want to live and just end up alive and not living.

Have you stopped to consider that just maybe God doesn't change our hard circumstances because He wants to give those hard situations time to change us?

He knows exactly what storm it will take to get out of us something He put in us. Ask yourself, "What exactly is God trying to teach me in my moments of adversity?"

Remember, God's plan is to ultimately get glory out of your life. Just like an olive has to be pressed to get oil, we will go through adversity. In the end, it will reveal His glory.

CHAPTER 3

⤸✖⤹

GRIEVING THE LIFE YOU THOUGHT YOU'D HAVE

As children, we imagine our lives turning out like a storybook fairy tale. My plan was to graduate high school, attend college, have a great career, get married, and have 2.5 children, a big house, and a fish tank. Nowhere in my plan did I remember penciling in *be diagnosed with lupus, get divorced, and go on disability*. Life threw me a curveball, and I was mad as hell because none of this was part of my plan.

When I should have been touring college campuses, I was getting tours of hospital emergency departments. When I should've been walking across a stage to get my college degree, I was learning to walk again with the aid of a walker. When I should've been caring for my own child, I was watching family members do it for me. I was sick of taking handfuls of medication for breakfast, lunch, and dinner.

I no longer recognized the former 121 pound woman because I had become a whopping 180 pounds and was still gaining. My life was out of control, and I felt helpless. It was like I was on a rollercoaster that took off at breakneck speed before I was able to brace myself.

I was physically, mentally, and emotionally spiraling out of control. I was sitting on a boat in the middle of a storm called grief, and the scary part was that I didn't have the sense to call on Jesus to calm the storm.

In the Mark 4:37-39 there is a story about the disciples being on a boat while Jesus was asleep. A storm came, and they were so afraid that they asked him if he cared that they were about to drown. This is where I was mentally.

I was grieving and drowning. You do not have to be experiencing the physical death of a loved one to be grieving. Elisabeth Kübler-Ross helps explain what grief is and its stages in her 1969 book, *On Death and Dying*. The stages of grief are:

- Denial: a defense mechanism that buffers the immediate shock of loss, numbing us to our emotions. We block out words and circumstances to try to hide from the facts.

- Anger: a strong feeling of annoyance, displeasure, or hostility aimed at inanimate objects, complete strangers, friends or family.

- Bargaining: the attempt to make a deal with God to postpone the inevitable and the accompanying pain to try to protect us from a painful reality.

- Depression: self-pity and feelings of loneliness, isolation, emptiness, and anxiety.

- Acceptance: emptiness we feel when we realize a person or situation is gone or over. In this stage, you might withdraw from life, feel numb, live in a fog, and not want to get out of bed.

I didn't necessarily go through the stages in the same order or experience all of them.

I went through these stages more than once and in no particular order. With some good makeup and a cute outfit, I concealed my emotions behind my famous "I'm fine" mask.

You know the one we wear when we want to look and act like we have it all together. The only person I was fooling was myself. I was a ticking time bomb that threw more temper tantrums than a room of sleepy 2-year-olds who had missed nap time.

I begged and pleaded with God to take this illness away and that I would do whatever He wanted. I tried so many things that only put a temporary bandage on what I was going through--alcohol, marijuana, pain pills, sex, and food-- but, none of them worked.

In fact, they only left me worse off with more issues than I started off with.

Soon, those feelings rushed right back in like a tsunami. I needed help because this hole was so deep that I didn't even look for the light anymore. But God has a way of surrounding you with people who are praying for you when you don't have the energy to fight anymore. Those people saw me drowning and threw out a lifeline for me. It is so important to have people who will speak truth to you and love you while you are in your mess.

At my church we call it "loving people to life."

That's just what they did.

Who's in your circle loving you to life? We each need those people in our lives who we can laugh and cry with. You don't know who you have in your circle until adversity hits. You will lose some friends when it seems like you're in the fight of your life, but take heart. It's God just shaking away those who are not fit for the fight.

If God had a way of reaching down in the midst of all that darkness to pull me out, He can and will do the same for you. We must come to understand that God has a plan for our lives that is greater than anything we can imagine for ourselves.

He knew before He formed you in your mother's womb that you were going to go through something that would change your life forever. In His infinite wisdom, He has also assigned people to come along and assist you in your toughest moments. He knew this beforehand, and He still has an assignment for you. I challenge you to embrace the life you have and let go of the life you have imagined.

In this season, God is doing a new thing. I don't want you to miss it because you are so focused on what should've happened or who left. You are still here and breathing, so there is still hope.

CHAPTER 4

❧

YOU ARE NOT EXEMPT

With all you're experiencing, I bet you're wondering, "Why me?"

Why not you? Just because you are walking with God doesn't mean you will be exempt from any of the storms of life. Actually, it makes you a target. The enemy knows that if he can distract you with storms, you will never lead anyone to Christ or be a living epistle.

I went in for a bone density test because my doctor had previously said I was showing signs of early onset osteoporosis due to the lupus diagnosis. A few days later, I received a call to come in and discuss my results. Just as the doctor had suspected, the osteoporosis had gotten worse. She wanted me to begin a medication that was supposed to slow down the process, as well as take vitamin D and calcium supplements. This medication would only be taken once a year by infusion. The day came, and I headed to the hospital. I wasn't really nervous because I used to get infusions monthly to treat lupus, so I knew the routine. Later that night, I felt sick at home. As with many medications, I expected there to be side effects, but these caught me by surprise. The next morning, I felt as if I was dying. I had hives on my legs, my joints were swollen, and my body felt like there was burning lava going through my veins. I immediately thought, "Oh my God, what have I done?" I called the number on the pamphlet they gave me, and I was instructed to go to the emergency room. Once I was there, I was told that there was nothing they could do for me because the medicine had to run its course. I would be lying if I said I wasn't ticked off.

"Here I go again," I thought to myself. I had been feeling the best I had felt in years, and now this happens. Why me, Lord? Why now? There I was laying in bed miserable. I could barely stand, had no appetite, and my entire body hurt. Not just for hours or a few days, but this went on for weeks. All of a sudden, the woman who had become independent was once again depending on her friends and family to care for her.

I had a lot of quiet time alone in my bed while my family members were at work and school. It was in those still moments that God was able to speak to me about the condition of my heart. I had not realized that there were things that I had been holding on to that were causing my heart to become hardened.

Sometimes when storms last longer than we would like, our hearts can get hard or angry. We can feel like we are the only one who suffers and end up growing resentful of others who seem to have it easier than us.

God doesn't allow the difficult trials and situations to stay in our lives to make us hard and angry. He does it to reveal our true condition. He knows exactly what we need, when we need it. It's also a reminder that in everything, He is in control. As long as you trust Him, it will work out for your good. As I reflected on all the times God brought me out, I realized that His track record was perfect. He had never failed and can't fail.

CHAPTER 5

⁂

PURPOSE REVEALED THROUGH PAIN

L osing all of my hair at the age of 7 to alopecia and living with lupus for more than 20 years revealed a lot about my character and the meaning of longsuffering.

I endured two bilateral hip replacements before the age of 35. I developed steroid-induced diabetes and high blood pressure, fibromyalgia, and osteoporosis. This would be enough to make the average person fold. I could've allowed all that happened to hinder me, but instead God used that pain to reveal my purpose.

I had no idea how much greatness was inside of me. We have to come to a place where we are able to minister out of our pain. The more we study the Word of God, go to church, attend Bible study, and get involved with life groups, the more we should grow.

This gave me the encouragement and strength I needed to reach out to others who were also living with lupus and alopecia. God used me to bring others hope. I still have my own personal battles, but I am determined not to let them stop me.

After my second hip replacement, I became a support group facilitator for the Lupus Foundation North Carolina Chapter. Soon, I was an advocate traveling to Capitol Hill to lobby for more funds for lupus research. I was blessed to conduct workshops, volunteer at events, hold fundraisers, and encourage others with lupus.

Not only was I blessed to educate the community about lupus, but I began ministering to women with alopecia. I have organized two "Bald is Beautiful" photo shoots with women who also are living with alopecia.

As you can see, it took that pain for God to reveal to me just how He was setting me up for greatness. That's not to say I wasn't tired, but it honestly gave me life. I knew that every time I told my story, I could also tell people of the goodness of God. Nothing you go through is in vain, nor is it wasted. Each experience has a lesson. God wants to show you just what He can do in you and through you, even in the storm.

CHAPTER 6

❧

ON THE OTHER SIDE

Psalm 41:3 writes, "The Lord sustains him on his sickbed; in his illness you restore him to full health."

Do you believe in miracles? If you recall in a previous chapter, I mentioned that I lived with lupus for more than 20 years. I know that according to the doctors and information on lupus that there's no cure for the disease. There was no special medication, particular hospital, or doctor. It wasn't a cure. I was healed. Yes, God still performs miracles. How do I know? I'm the recipient of one.

I'm a country girl that loves being outdoors. I love fishing, planting flowers, and walking. These were all things I could not do while I was sick because the heat from the sun would send me into a lupus flare or cause my skin to break out.

One day I decided that I wanted a miniature rose bush with some other flowers and red mulch. I jumped in my car and went to a local gardening store to purchase what I needed.

I was kind of afraid because I started to think about how my body was going to react doing all of that yard work on such a warm, sunny day. I made up my mind that I was going to trust the fact I was healed as God had said.

It took me three days to get rid of all the weeds, dig the holes for the plants, and spread the mulch. It was hard work, and boy was I tired. Guess what? I did not get sick!

No flares. No rash. Nothing.

Trust in God.

People wonder how I know I'm healed or that the disease is in remission. All I know is that I don't know how or why God did it, but I'm grateful He did.

My doctor doesn't even ask me about it when I go for checkups. I have not had an abnormal lab result in four years, except for the normal vitamin deficiencies.

There are no aches, no pain, no diabetes, no high blood pressure, and no fibromyalgia.

NOTHING. Trust me, there was nothing I did to deserve healing. But, if God has to show His glory in someone, why not me? And why not you?

CHAPTER 7

RESTORATION

Joel 2:25-26 says, "'I will restore to you the years that the swarming locust has eaten, the hopper, the destroyer, and the cutter, my great army, which I sent among you. You shall eat in plenty and be satisfied, and praise the name of the LORD your God, who has dealt wondrously with you. And my people shall never again be put to shame.'"

I have my life back.

It was as if God pressed the reset button and granted me a do-over. I now work full-time and live alone. My health is better than it has ever been and, more importantly, God is allowing me to use my story to draw the lost to Him and give others hope.

I will never understand why God chose me -- all I know is that He did.

I want everything I do and say to ignite hope in others. I want people to understand that even if God does not heal them physically, His grace is sufficient to get them through any storm that might arise.

If you stop and think about it, you have made it 100% out of every storm thus far. If you are indeed a child of God, I want you to trust and believe that He has a plan for your life to restore everything that the enemy has stolen from you. Not only has my health been restored, my purpose was revealed.

I pray that as you have read just a glimpse of some of the amazing things God has been able to do in my life when it felt like I was sinking in despair, you have begun to hope again.

God doesn't play favorites. Surely, if He can restore a life that felt like it was doomed for 20 years, He can truly do it for you.

EPILOGUE

How do we know if we have faith if it is never tested?

If every day is sunny, our children are acting like they have sense, we're getting along with our spouse, and there's plenty of money in the bank, how would we ever know how strong our faith is?

Faith is like a muscle--in order for it to grow, it has to be exercised.

Adversity is designed to purify us and develop patience and character. It has a way of showing us what we really believe deep down. It's easy to sing about God being our Savior, Healer, and Deliverer until we have to be saved, healed, and delivered.

We can be thankful for our trials because, once we've passed through them, we have tangible evidence of our faith. In this way, our trials do us a great service in giving us confidence that we are not just fooling ourselves but really believe in Christ.

ABOUT THE AUTHOR/ CONNECT WITH ME LINKS

website TamekaJoyner.com

IG: TlJoyner

FB: Tameka Joyner

BIO

Tameka Joyner is the eldest daughter of five children. Raised in a single-parent home, she learned how to care for others, which helped develop her compassion for the sick and hurting. When she lost her hair at 7, she endured extreme bullying for years. As a result, she learned how to hide in plain sight and not draw any attention to herself. She was diagnosed with lupus when she was just a teen. She had no idea that when her faith walk with God began at the age of 33, everything she had known would change. She went from allowing illness to steal her voice to taking back her power and using her voice to inspire hope in others.

www.ingramcontent.com/pod-product-compliance
Lightning Source LLC
Chambersburg PA
CBHW031221090426
42740CB00009B/1258